Spotlight

Laura Da Costa

BookLeaf
Publishing

Presentation by *BookLeaf Publishing*

Web: www.bookleafpub.com

E-mail: info@bookleafpub.com

ISBN: 9789357441506

First edition 2023

To

Skye, for her endless support and caffeine supply,

Paxton, for choosing us,

and Freddie, for being the best baking partner ever.

ACKNOWLEDGEMENT

I would never have signed up to this challenge without encouragement from my fiancé, Skye, my sister, Sofia, and my brother-in-law, Kurtis. We all signed up to it together, which has made this process a fun and competitive rollercoaster. Thank you for pushing me out of my comfort zone and making me realise that I really would have regretted not doing this!

I Am Not A Morning Person

Shreek!
There it goes again.
Really need caffeine.

Paxton has pushed things off the table
again
Ingrained into our routine.

Maybe if I annoy them enough, they will snap
out of their laziness
and give me my food?
Calculations of a cat.

I feel something prodding
and then digging
at my face.
The sharp cherry on top,
just in case.

Paxton's Room

It has been a while
Since I chased and wondered and prowled and
hissed
and existed as I should.
Within this tiny room that is worlds away from
how things used to be, I wonder
When will I next chase some mice? Where is my
food? Will someone visit me
more than once a day?
Paw needs cleaning, I'm hungry, someone give
me fresh water, will they take me home next
time?
Why did they not want me?
I'm perfect.

Was it something I did? Will they come back?
Itchy leg, bite it better. Bite bite bite with
affection,
maybe one day someone will understand.

Another one came today, and another and
another the other day
I think
but that was all and nothing more.

Oh what's this? Visitors!
Jump, meow, play, bite, repeat
Maybe they will want me.

Twilight Food

Food time is constant
right?
Meow at the humans
until they agree.
Always is the perfect time
They love me. I'm invincible.
Snuggle into her armpit, maybe
some manipulation
will speed this up.

That didn't work.
Phase 2, knock useless things off the table.
Movement, yes!
Oh, nevermind. Time to deploy

The Paw on Face.

I sense progress.
They shuffle reluctantly
such well-trained pets.
I lead the way, just in case they have forgotten.
And I finally,
finally,
get my way.
As always.

Banana Cake

Banana cake!
He waddles confidently to the kitchen, leading
the way
Cake it is.

Something about experiencing the everyday
through the eyes of a child
injects an enchanting aura into normality
Mundane things suddenly burst with exuberance
and colour
completely pure and uncomplicated.

Mash mash mash, good job!
A teaspoon of baking powder, oh! That
was probably three
Rise and continue, it will all work out
Flour clouds the air, eventually raining into the
bowl,
and onto most of the kitchen
Crack! And release the shell, it falls in too
Several glugs of vanilla and an eruption of
cinnamon later, we

Mix mix mix, good job! All done!

The pedantic particularity of measuring
ingredients
quickly becomes redundant when you
accidentally realise
it hardly makes a difference at all.

Mum and Cake

Do you want to make a cake?
Yes!
Okay, you mix.

It filled me with warmth, the simplest kind.
That crinkled, faded notebook, curated with
antiques
pages leaping with timeless goods
I wonder where that went?

The process, company, quality time
Illusive mess that evaporated instantly
Measuring ingredients? Ha, not me
this looks about right
and somehow it was, every time.
Mix until you see the air bubbles,
that looks about right

That book was overflowing with recipes
an heirloom, faded with time.
We alternated between the same 6 or 7
Pineapple-upside-down, yogurt, orange,
chocolate with creamy coconut
Childhood flavours
If I think hard enough I can taste them all.

Can I lick the bowl?
Yes, but you'll make yourself sick.

I still did it.

Returning to the Island

Transported through shudders and waves
Suddenly
We turn
and the island glides majestically into sight.
Glimmering and waving, recognising familiar
faces.

We step outside
Lulled and embraced by the salty, earthy air
Swaddled by the warmth and brilliance of the
sun
explosions of colour and familiarity
guide and cradle us along.

Back at last
we all think,
faces plastered with relaxed, gaping smiles.

Community

Bom dia!
I jerk and reply mechanically, awed and startled
That would never happen in Streatham.

We arrive
bundles of gifts greet us at the door
potatoes, grapes, passion fruits, figs
Affectionately engulfed by the comfort
of home grown food from neighbours.

We wonder
through roads that we know well
overflowing with memories and the warmth of
familiar faces.
Dogs follow curiously, intrigued
by the scent of these familiar strangers.

Blanket of Stars

Lie on the balcony and look up at infinity
Lose yourself.
Consume yourself in that blanket of darkness
sprinkled generously with thousands, millions of
lights.

What can you see?
A bear, stalking purposefully into a
cat glaring and licking her paw next to a
little boy playing with a ball and a
monkey, trying to catch it? What a scene!

Look up for hours and overwhelm yourself with
inspiration
immerse yourself, without distractions, in the
awesome vastness of
her psychedellic beauty
of the stories and perspectives that she gifts
Unique to all
who remember to look.

Blink and the story fades
a choreographed replacement dances forward
timed immaculately to take its place.
An infinite cycle

as long as you remember
to look.

Transported

Monopoly, was that the first?
So destructive, surprising that it wasn't also the
last.

Can we play?
Okay.

Time froze and flew,
fuelled by competitiveness, agitation, and the
sharp discomfort
of that hard wood floor.

Over time, we migrated to the dining table.
The stack grew, and so did the playing field.
We adventured through portals of meeples,
playdough, letters, meteors, bamboo, lakes,
planets
Built cities card by round
Even responded to pandemics, before reality
intervened.

Later, Spotify carried us further
into the magical depths of different worlds.
The underlying spirit remained:
Must

Not
Lose.
But it's okay,
Jorge usually loses anyway.

The Football Pitch

The bell jolts us to break
Time to play!

We scramble and race to the pitch
Who has the ball? Hurry,
filter into teams and go

What do you want to be when you grow up?
That question was easy
Football consumed my mind, everything I
wanted to do
and be

Remember
Games outside the estate, in the park
Always the only girl, but that never crossed my
mind then
or anyone else's
it just was.

And then things changed
Consumed instead by doubts and questions of
possibility
Stopped overlooking, started noticing

ingrained behaviours that were probably always
there.
Football players do not look or act or seem like
me
and what was once unquestionable ran far away
from reality.

Unfamiliar

Time to go.
Pack up your life into two suitcases
pick only what you can carry.
That excludes Merlin and Luna, by the way.

Something fresh, a challenge!
This was my choice, I remind myself
with dread

A train a coach, a flash of green
We arrive
to the unfamiliar freshness of country air
A sea of faces enter the scene, all gasping for
interaction and connection.

"Oh look, I have black Vans too!"
I nod too quickly and smile unnaturally,
eager and desperate to find any common ground.

My things barely fill the space
They disappear, like me, into unfamiliarity
making things feel larger and colder
than they should.
Must buy some oversized, useless things
to plaster this emptiness.

The Haze

March 23
Two or three weeks and things will return to
normal
so they said.

Everything from that time was a haze
Time travelled poorly, and often not at all
What happened last week?
The heavy weight of nothing, once again.

In pairs we walked and said hello to some sheep
Wrote on a TV once a day and deceived
ourselves
with vibrant colours
Virtual mother's day celebrations and birthdays
to maintain a warmth that we all craved
but could not quite reach

Tried to say hello to the sea
but it also retreated.
Follow the rules and we will all be safe,
so they said.

After a lifetime, things "returned to normal"
How can anything ever be normal again?

One Walk Per Day

Walking was freedom
However fleeting.
It connected us to nature and others and
ourselves
Rooted while everything
fell apart

One walk per day, make it count.
That was our currency, spend it wisely
What was once unquestionable, inflated.
No longer taken for granted.

Clap every Thursday, after your walk
Appreciate the little things and avoid being
swallowed
by emptiness
Cling to that tranquil, cleansing
daily walk
and start again the next day.

Imposter

Fake it until you become it
or something
Probably need to remember that phrase first.

Aim everywhere and something will land
when you get somewhere, just pretend some
more
We all do it.

"It was luck" or "I had a lot of help"
Why is it so natural to deflect success?
In this virtual room of brilliance
when will someone notice that I am the odd one
out?

So what do you think?
I conjure up a monologue that sounds
vaguely acceptable.
Everyone nods thoughtlessly
as if instructed to do so.

And I daydream
about what I would rather be doing instead.

If I Could

Daydreams swirl, cataloguing visions of how
things could be.

Travelling the world and transporting myself
through customs, flavours, landscapes
Challenging myself with unusual, terrifying,
wonderful experiences
Broadening my vision
with a wealth of perspectives.

Opening a cafe
Crumbling over volatility and loving every
second
Assuming control but relenting it too, to factors
beyond mine.
Documented, worldwide flavours would be
tools,
workshopped into unique hybrids
blending together the best from all.

Hosting workshops seasonally
to share my creations and hybrid secrets
with my small, whole world.

There would also be cats, obviously,

and the pitter patter
of tiny feet.

Unpredictable

People's faces give a lot away.
A raised eyebrow, stares, glares, scowls,
the occasional grin.
Head up to the sky and ignore it all
Much easier that way.

Holding someone's hand is a privilege
A daily victory for a battle
not yet won,
A relentless calculation of benefit versus risk,
An incessant temperature check with
unpredictable errors,
fluctuating at every step.
It is an unwanted spotlight
with no off switch.

It is also perspective
So many are not this lucky,
and we would be grateful,
if that was enough.

This should not require such complex
consideration.
It should just be
without the occasional

"Why don't you jump off a bridge?"

Does my existence upset you?
I'm truly sorry
that you are so fragile.

Revenge

There is something freeing and validating
about walking among others who live like you.
An unspoken understanding, no pretending, no
hiding
only being
and believing
in something bright.

Safety, acceptance, warmth, confidence
fearlessness,
however fleeting,
emerge from hibernation and lead the way
gracing me temporarily with their presence.
This is my revenge.

Magic

Filled with dread
and roast potatoes, cheese, wine, baileys
Who knows what else.
Back to bland.

Time raced.
Eagerly waiting
by the window for the family to arrive.
Warmth, magic, laughter, board games, the
token broken glass
paper hats that never seem to fit.
Counting the minutes to midnight but never
wanting the day to end

It is all a glittery, fragrant, enchanting haze, yet
it retreats back into boxes suddenly, without
delay
dormant once again until it is time.

Happy New Year! They slur
as everyone turns blue
Deceiving the world and themselves too.
Here is 50% off our gym membership, an
exclusive,
just for you!

I'm on my knees with gratitude.
Ambushed by relentless
forced
optimism
to plaster the blues.

9 789357 441506